CONTENTS

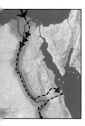
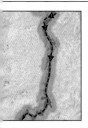
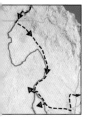
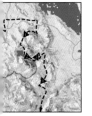
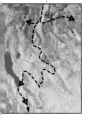

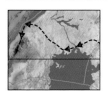
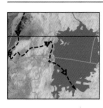
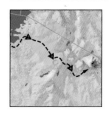
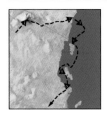
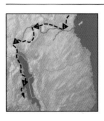

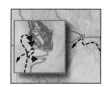

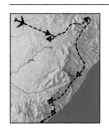
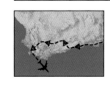
Key

 route

 place visited

 national park/ game reserve

 country border

 river

THE PYRAMIDS & SPHINX

We start our journey in the exciting and colourful city of Cairo. With over 15 million people it is Africa's biggest city, and it sits in a unique position at the cross-roads of Africa, Asia, and Europe.

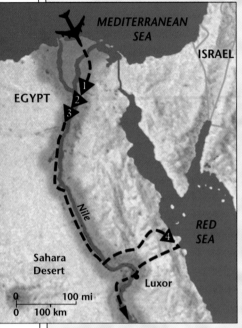

The Cairo Tower provides a bird's-eye view of the bustling city from a balcony 187 metres high. To one side are the alleys and bazaars of the old city and to the other the office blocks, banks, hotels, and wide streets of the new city. The pyramids at Giza dominate the view to the west. Our first stop is the Egyptian Museum. If you looked carefully you would see this next to the chaotic bus station to the east of the tower. For our second stop we explore a fascinating bazaar in Cairo and then travel southwest to the pyramids at Giza. Lastly, we head east to the Red Sea.

MUSEUM STOP

Egyptian Antiquities

The Museum of Egyptian Antiquities holds over 100,000 exhibits. It would take over nine months to see all of them if you looked at each for just one minute. Walking through the treasure-filled rooms, lined with sphinxes and statues of ancient Egyptian gods, you can imagine you have travelled back in time. The treasures of the boy-king, Tutankhamun, are the highlight of the museum. They include his gold funeral mask inlaid with blue gemstones. Tutankhamun reigned from c.1333 BC for only about nine years.

Cairo

Cairo is famous for bazaars (Arabic markets) and Khan El Khalili is one of the biggest and best in the world. Weaving through the maze of alleys you can bargain with traders for anything from shoes to copper to spices to souvenirs. Keep a special look-out for craftsmen making beautiful jewellery or useful pots and pans. In the 'Street of Gold' you will find many traditional craftsmen hammering and polishing gold,

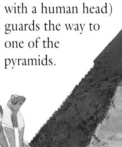

The pyramids and the sphinx

The pyramids at Giza are considered one of the Seven Wonders of the World. The Great Pyramid of Cheops is the biggest, standing 137 metres high and made from over 2,000,000 giant stone blocks. You can climb inside along steep tunnels and find ancient burial chambers – some big enough to hold a double-decker bus! A camel ride takes you to the sphinx. The stone sphinx (a lion's body with a human head) guards the way to one of the pyramids.

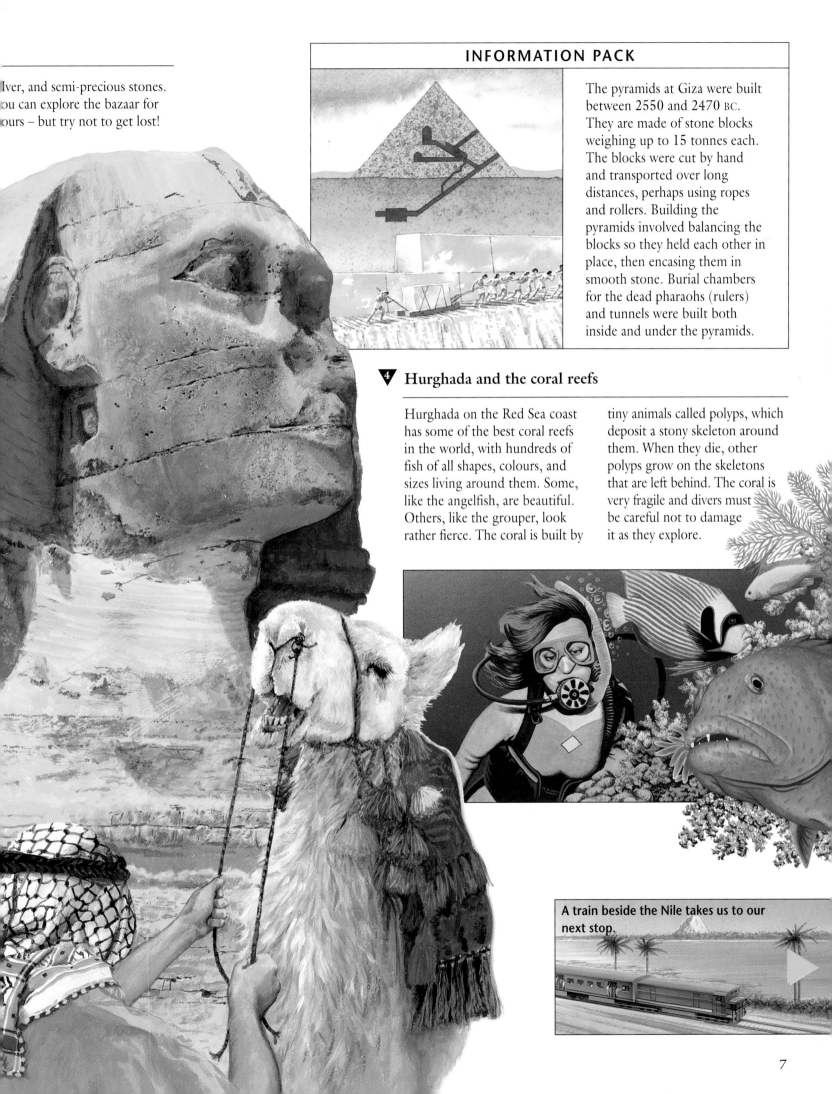

lver, and semi-precious stones.
ou can explore the bazaar for
ours – but try not to get lost!

INFORMATION PACK

The pyramids at Giza were built between 2550 and 2470 BC. They are made of stone blocks weighing up to 15 tonnes each. The blocks were cut by hand and transported over long distances, perhaps using ropes and rollers. Building the pyramids involved balancing the blocks so they held each other in place, then encasing them in smooth stone. Burial chambers for the dead pharaohs (rulers) and tunnels were built both inside and under the pyramids.

▼ Hurghada and the coral reefs

Hurghada on the Red Sea coast has some of the best coral reefs in the world, with hundreds of fish of all shapes, colours, and sizes living around them. Some, like the angelfish, are beautiful. Others, like the grouper, look rather fierce. The coral is built by tiny animals called polyps, which deposit a stony skeleton around them. When they die, other polyps grow on the skeletons that are left behind. The coral is very fragile and divers must be careful not to damage it as they explore.

A train beside the Nile takes us to our next stop.

THE RIVER NILE

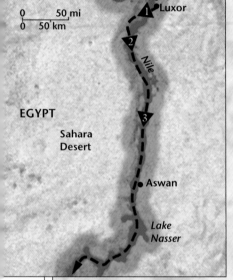

0 50 mi
0 50 km

Luxor

Nile

EGYPT

Sahara
Desert

Aswan

Lake
Nasser

Leaving the train at Luxor we head through the town and take a ferry across the Nile to another resting place of the great pharaohs – the Valley of the Kings. The many tombs in this valley once held the bodies and treasures of Egyptian kings and queens but most have been robbed, so we cannot be too sure of what they contained. Some believe there may still be undiscovered tombs full of treasures like those of Tutankhamun.

After the heat and dust of the valley a relaxing boat trip on the Nile is just what you need. You can watch life drift past and view grand temples like those of Karnak and Hatshepsut. You may also see farmers looking after their crops beside the river. Our last stop shows us how local people use the Nile to water their crops using traditional techniques. The journey then continues down the Nile towards Aswan and Lake Nasser.

▶ The Temple of Hatshepsut

Relaxing on a felucca (a traditional Egyptian boat) is a magical experience and drifting up and down the majestic Nile, fringed with palm trees and the mighty limestone cliffs of the West Bank, you may feel like a pharaoh yourself. From the felucca you can see people on the banks washing clothes, bathing, watering animals, and fetching water for crops or cooking. You soon realize how important the river is to those living near it.

As you drift upstream from Luxor you will see the magnificent temple of Queen Hatshepsut, the first female pharaoh, who was born in c. 1540 BC. From a distance the terraced temple looks as though it is carved from the Theban mountains that surround it. It was discovered about a hundred years ago and is still being restored today.

The Valley of the Kings

n this hot sandy valley lie the mbs of pharaohs. It was here, 1922, that Tutankhamun's easures were discovered. As ou enter Tutankhamun's tomb ou can imagine what it looked ke filled with his treasures, hich you saw earlier in the gyptian Museum. The burial hamber walls are painted with ctures of Egyptian gods and ncient Egyptian writing nown as hieroglyphics.

The Egyptians believed that after they died their bodies should be preserved to ensure life after death. To preserve, or mummify, a body most of the organs were removed, the body was treated with salts and spices, wrapped in cloth, and finally put in a sarcophagus (coffin). Some of these bodies are still complete after more than 3,000 years.

3 The shaduf

Irrigation is the process of adding water to crops and is most often used in hot dry areas that have little rainfall. Irrigation methods vary from modern computer-controlled pipe networks to older systems of canals and sluice gates. You will notice many Egyptian farmers using a shaduf. The shaduf has been used for hundreds of years and is simply a bucket attached to a long pole with a weight at the other end. The farmer lowers the bucket into the river and the weight on the other end helps lift the heavy bucket up again. The water is then emptied into a channel that carries it to the fields.

From Aswan we board a ferry for the trip down Lake Nasser.

THE NUBIAN DESERT

Heading south on Lake Nasser it becomes very hot and temperatures can reach nearly 50°C before the cooling rains of July and August arrive. About 280 kilometres south of Aswan the ferry passes Abu Simbel, the site of the Great Temple of Ramses II, before crossing into Sudanese waters and docking at Wadi Halfa.

Sudan is enormous (it is the biggest country in Africa). Its landscape varies dramatically from the central grasslands to the deserts of the north to the marshes of the Sudd in the south. First we cross the rocks and dust of the Nubian Desert (an extension of the Sahara) using a souq, which is a Sudanese goods lorry. We then stop to explore the pyramids and temples of the ancient Meroe Kingdom. The capital, Khartoum, and its sister city, Omdurman, will be our next stops. Then we will visit one of the largest farms in the world.

3 Royal City of Meroe

The Royal City of Meroe was once the capital of the Nubian Kingdom of Kush (538 BC to AD 350), famous for its iron industry and advanced agriculture. The Nubians were similar to the Egyptians but had their own language and hieroglyphics, which are still not fully understood. All that is left of the Kush kingdom today are the tall pyramid tombs and the temples of Musawwarat and Naqa at Meroe. Look at the style of these temples and you may notice that the Egyptians, Romans, and Greeks influenced the Meroe architecture.

▼ 1 Abu Simbel and Lake Nasser

The Great Temple of Ramses II at Abu Simbel is one of the most impressive temples in Egypt. It was in danger of being lost under Lake Nasser when the Aswan High Dam, built in 1960, blocked the Nile and flooded the valley in which it stood. Luckily, a team of experts cut the 3,200-year-old temple into over 2,000 giant blocks and rebuilt it above the rising lake.

Gezira

l Jazirah, better known as ezira, is a giant farming area etween the White Nile and the lue Nile, famous for its cotton lantations. Cotton is Sudan's ajor crop and export and the

Gezira region provides about 70 per cent of Sudan's total production. Sorghum, vegetables, and wheat are also grown to feed Sudan's population.

▼ The Twin Cities

At the point where the White Nile and the Blue Nile meet, the city of Omdurman looks over the water to the Sudanese capital, Khartoum. Founded in 1821 Khartoum grew rapidly because of the region's slave trade and became the capital city in 1834. It is a quiet modern city. Omdurman, on the other side of the river, is completely different and appears to have been left behind by time. The narrow dusty alleys winding between mud houses are bustling with life. The focus is the bazaar (market), which is the biggest in Sudan. A visit to the Hamed an-Niel Mosque just before sunset on a Friday would enable you to see the Sufi whirling dervishes, who dance and chant in prayer to their sheikh (Islamic leader).

◀ Crossing the Nubian Desert

Travelling between towns and villages in Sudan can be difficult because of the harsh desert environment and the great distances that are often involved. Souq lorries are the most common means of transport. They transport everything. Climbing aboard you could be sharing the space with goats, sacks of grain, bales of cotton, and as many as 30 people. The journey is not comfortable and often long and tiring, but it is a truly Sudanese experience. The thick dust clouds that swirl across the desert and savanna, and the searing heat mean you need plenty of water.

Another souq lorry takes us past the mountains of Kassala to Eritrea.

THE SOURCE OF THE NILE

When we think of Ethiopia we often think of the terrible famines that were shown on television all over the world. Many of us imagine a country of deserts and no water, but in reality Ethiopia is very fertile in parts and is dominated not by deserts but by large mountains.

After passing through Eritrea we reach Ethiopia for our first stop. This involves a hike into the Simien mountains to see some stunning scenery and rare wildlife. Then we visit the impressive Tis Abay Falls, where the Blue Nile begins its long journey through Sudan and Egypt to the sea. Climbing into the mountains again, we stop at the rock-carved churches of Lalibela. Then passing through the capital, Addis Ababa, we experience the epiphany ceremony, which is the most important celebration of the Ethiopian Orthodox Church.

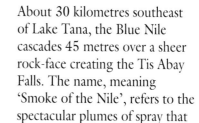

2 The Tis Abay Falls

About 30 kilometres southeast of Lake Tana, the Blue Nile cascades 45 metres over a sheer rock-face creating the Tis Abay Falls. The name, meaning 'Smoke of the Nile', refers to the spectacular plumes of spray that look like smoke rising from a fire.

The falls are made up of several sections separated by rocky islands covered in lush vegetation that clings to the edge. Though not as big as Victoria Falls in Zimbabwe, Tis Abay Falls are beautiful to look at, especially after the rainy season.

4 Addis Ababa

Just after Christmas, which falls on the 6th of January in Ethiopia, the Ethiopian Orthodox Church celebrates epiphany, known locally as *timkat*. This is their most important ceremony, celebrating the baptism of Christ in the river Jordan. It is centred around Lalibela but also takes place elsewhere, including the capital, Addis Ababa. Holy tablets of stone called tabots, representing the original tablets from the Ark of the Covenant, are wrapped in silk and then carried on the heads of priests, sheltered by velvet umbrellas representing the heavens.

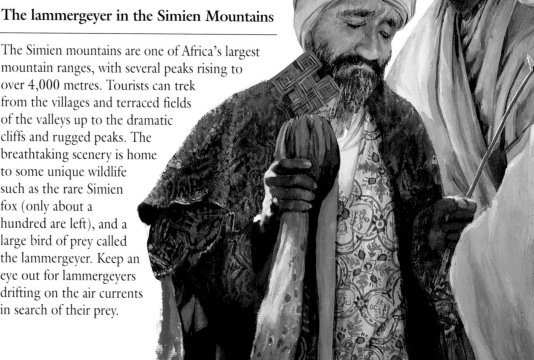

1 The lammergeyer in the Simien Mountains

The Simien mountains are one of Africa's largest mountain ranges, with several peaks rising to over 4,000 metres. Tourists can trek from the villages and terraced fields of the valleys up to the dramatic cliffs and rugged peaks. The breathtaking scenery is home to some unique wildlife such as the rare Simien fox (only about a hundred are left), and a large bird of prey called the lammergeyer. Keep an eye out for lammergeyers drifting on the air currents in search of their prey.

3 Lalibela

Set in the rugged Lasta mountains, Lalibela is known for its fascinating underground churches that were carved into the red stone hillsides some 800 years ago. It is said that King Lalibela gathered up to 40,000 of the world's finest craftsmen to carve them, in an effort to copy the biblical city of Jerusalem. The churches are still Christian shrines today, and if you follow the chants of gentle prayer you might find the white-robed hermits in their underground world.

INFORMATION PACK

Ethiopia has had several famines in the past twenty years in which an estimated two million people have starved to death. A famine normally occurs when the rains fail and the hot sun causes crops to wither and die, just as grass goes brown and dry without rain in the summer. Most countries solve this problem by moving food from areas where it has rained, but in Ethiopia a long and violent civil war prevented food reaching those who most needed it. International aid agencies, such as the Red Cross, struggled to get some food to the starving people. The war meant that many more people died than would otherwise have done.

We continue along the Great Rift Valley.

13

THE GREAT RIFT VALLEY

The Great Rift Valley cuts 24,000 kilometres across the face of east Africa like a giant gaping wound. Its mountains, lakes, deserts, and grasslands include the most spectacular scenery in Africa. The next stages of our journey are in or around the valley, taking you into this incredible landscape.

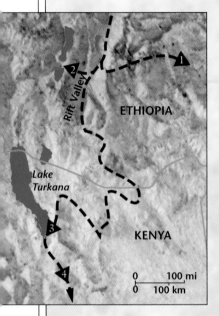

First we travel underground in the cool shade of the Sof Omar cave system to see the power of water shaping the land it flows through. Then we climb to the heights of Chencha to visit a Dorze settlement and take our first proper views over the Rift Valley below. Crossing into Kenya we stop at Lake Turkana, the world's biggest permanent desert lake, and meet the elegant Turkana people. We see how they live and consider their changing relationship with the environment. Following this we embark on a hair-raising jeep drive near the Losiolo escarpment and deep into the heart of the Valley.

The Sof Omar caves

The Sof Omar caves offer the ideal chance to escape the hot African sun. A river has cut through the soft limestone over thousands of years to create an enormous system of underground chambers and connecting tunnels. They extend for over 15 kilometres, making them one of the largest cave systems in the world.

Lake Turkana

The blue-green waters of Lake Turkana prompted early explorers to call it 'the Jade Sea', but its proper name refers to the Turkana people who live around its shores. They have had very little contact with other Kenyans, and continue to lead traditional lives as nomadic pastoralists. This life-style involves walking great distances in search of grass to feed their cattle, camels, and goats. When they move they take their belongings with them. Women can be seen carrying many of the things on their heads. Population growth has put pressure on the grazing lands so many Turkana have recently taken up fishing for extra food.

The Dorze of Chencha

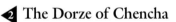

The village of Chencha in the highlands is well-known to many Ethiopians for its cooler weather. But at an altitude of 1,600 metres it provides fantastic views of the Rift Valley. The vegetation is dominated by large patches of bamboo and purple juniper shrubs, which can withstand the cooler weather. The local Dorze people use the bamboo to make their huts. The huts are sometimes 12 metres tall and, even though they are only made of bamboo, are very strong and last for up to 50 years.

INFORMATION PACK

Over millions of years violent earth movements have caused a large section of land to sink along two parallel fault lines, creating a massive trench. As the land sank, hot lava from deep in the earth was forced to the surface forming the volcanoes, mountains, lava pools, and hot lakes that you see today. The result of these actions is the Great Rift Valley.

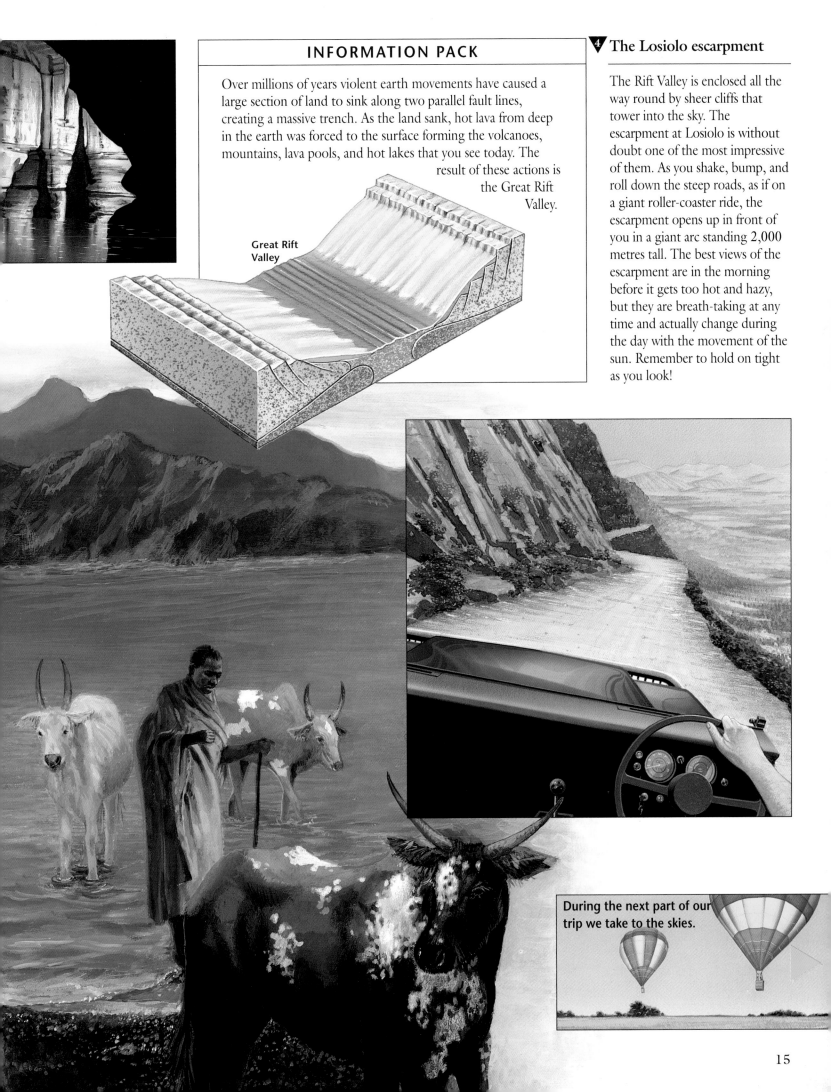

Great Rift Valley

▼ The Losiolo escarpment

The Rift Valley is enclosed all the way round by sheer cliffs that tower into the sky. The escarpment at Losiolo is without doubt one of the most impressive of them. As you shake, bump, and roll down the steep roads, as if on a giant roller-coaster ride, the escarpment opens up in front of you in a giant arc standing 2,000 metres tall. The best views of the escarpment are in the morning before it gets too hot and hazy, but they are breath-taking at any time and actually change during the day with the movement of the sun. Remember to hold on tight as you look!

During the next part of our trip we take to the skies.

THE GREAT MIGRATION

We have now arrived at the great plains area of Africa, where huge areas of savanna and scrub stretch as far as the eye can see. They are home to one of the greatest concentrations of wildlife on the planet, from the big bold mammals to the smallest and strangest insects. Our first stop is Samburu National Reserve, which stands as a fertile refuge in an otherwise dry landscape.

Following that, prepare for a change of climate as we take a challenging trek up Mount Kenya. We then descend into the Kenyan capital, Nairobi, to relax and take a short break from the wilderness. Here we can explore the city and learn about local cultures by visiting the Bomas of Kenya. Finally our journey takes to the air as we glide peacefully over the Maasai Mara for a unique and memorable view of the great wildebeest migration.

1 Samburu National Reserve

In the hot dry landscape around Mount Kenya lies Samburu National Reserve. It was made a national park in 1985 to protect wildlife living near the Ewaso Nyira River. Because of its remoteness it is one of the country's least visited reserves. Although it lacks some of the big game there is still plenty to see. Look out for local species like the reticulated giraffe, the Somali ostrich (which has blue legs instead of pink ones), and the bright orange-bellied parrot.

2 Mount Kenya

The second highest peak in Africa, Mount Kenya (5,199 metres) is actually an extinct volcano that provides good trekking for amateurs and tough climbing for experienced mountaineers. As you climb towards the permanently snow-capped peak you will notice the vegetation changing, and due to its position on the equator, you may spot unique plants growing on its slopes. Despite its position on the equator, Mount Kenya gets very cold at night and it often rains or even snows at higher altitudes. This means you have to carry proper equipment, which may slow you down.

3 The Luo Dance in Nairobi

Nairobi, the capital of Kenya, is a modern thriving city with a mixture of old and new. On the outskirts you will find the Bomas of Kenya, a display of Kenya's traditional homesteads (bomas). Each tribal group has its own building style. Having seen these you can relax and watch a traditional dancing display. Among the many different groups the Luo dancers are very colourful in their feathered head-dresses.

The Maasai Mara is Kenya's greatest wildlife reserve and one of the best in the world. Its scenes of animals seem to change every time you blink your eyes. From the ground the sights are amazing but to see this vast pool of life properly you need a bird's-eye view from a hot air balloon. High up in the air you watch life unfold as the animals busily graze, hunt, and rear their young. In July each year one of the world's greatest migrations begins as millions of wildebeest arrive in the reserve from Tanzania. They come north with the rains so that they can feed on the fresh grass, moving back to the Serengeti in Tanzania when the rains return there.

INFORMATION PACK

Across Africa many national parks and reserves have been set up to protect the local environment and the wildlife that depends upon it. Park wardens keep hunters away and stop tourists damaging the reserves. For example, the wardens have stopped many elephants from being killed for their ivory tusks.

Next a jeep takes us on through the savanna woodland.

THE SANCTUARY FOR RHINOS

We are now in the highlands, whose rich soils, warm temperatures, good sunshine, and plentiful rain make it one of Kenya's central farming regions. It is here that Europeans set up vast coffee and tea estates, pushing the local Kikuyu people off the land they had farmed for hundreds of years. It is here also that the Mau Mau independence movement started as the Kikuyu people fought to regain their land from the British. Our first stop in this area is at a tea estate near Kericho, Kenya's tea capital. We then head back through the Rift Valley to the famous soda lake at Nakuru, where thousands of flamingos can be seen wading in its waters. We then visit a rhinoceros sanctuary that has been a local success story in the battle to save Kenya's wildlife from human hunters. Finally we stop at a great imaginary line – the equator – which is signposted by the roadside, before heading into Uganda.

UGANDA

KENYA

Malaba

equator

Nairobi

0   100 mi
0   100 km

▶ Kericho

Kericho is Kenya's tea capital. The fertile soils and good climate, with guaranteed rains almost every afternoon, make this the most important tea-growing region in Africa. Kenya is the fourth biggest producer of tea in the world, and nearly everyone living near Kericho is involved in the industry. You will see people picking, withering, mashing, soaking, and drying the tea leaves before they are packed into wooden tea-chests and shipped across the world. Before leaving, try a cup at the Tea Hotel!

▼ 2 The pink lake

Lake Nakuru is a beautiful national park. In Swahili Nakuru means 'place of the waterbuck' and as the name suggests there are several thousand of these antelopes here. But the lake is better known for its huge flocks of flamingos that seem to turn the water and skies pink as they move. You can watch them as they turn their heads upside down in the water to feed on algae and plankton, using their specially shaped bills. There are two types of flamingo here – the lesser flamingo and the greater flamingo, which can grow as tall as a small person.

▼3 The Rhino Sanctuary

Many of Africa's animals are under threat from human populations who use the land they live on. Others are threatened by hunting such as the leopard, hunted for its skin, and the elephant, hunted for its ivory tusks. This illegal hunting (poaching) is especially dangerous for the rhinoceros population. Their horns are often used in Chinese traditional medicine and to make dagger handles in Yemen. As a result of this illegal trade, Kenya's rhino population has fallen from about 20,000 in 1970 to less than 350 in 1983. Now there is hope that the rhino will be saved, thanks to conservation groups like Rhino Rescue. Conservation groups have helped set up a sanctuary at Lake Nakuru that has electric fences and armed guards to keep the hunters out. Here the rhinos are safe and, as their numbers increase, perhaps other sanctuaries will be set up in Kenya.

INFORMATION PACK

In many parts of the world, animals and their environments are in danger from the activities of humans. This is particularly true for Africa's wildlife. The concern for these endangered animals has led several groups to try to save them. Two important groups are the International Fund for Animal Welfare (IFAW) and the World Wide Fund for Nature (WWF).

To find out more about these organizations, you can contact them directly:

IFAW, Warren Court, Park Road, Crowborough, TN6 2GA

WWF, Panda House, Weyside Park, Catteshall Lane, Godalming GU7 1XR.

▼4 The equator

On the journey northwest you might pass a sign by the roadside telling you that you are on the equator. The equator is the imaginary line around the centre of the earth (0° latitude), at an equal distance from the north and south poles. On and near the equator the hours of daylight are the same length all year. Further from the equator, for example in Europe, the days are shorter in winter and longer in summer.

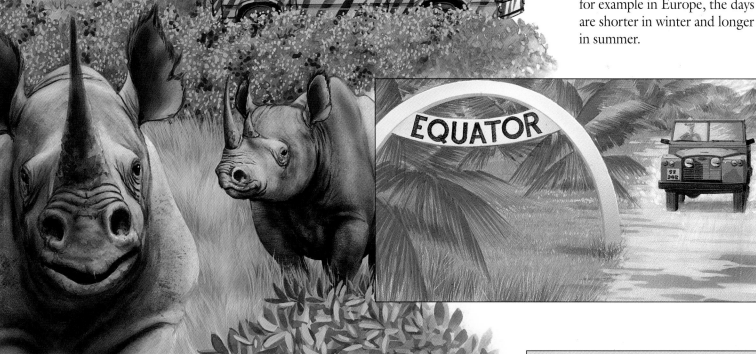

We continue with a train journey to Malaba.

THE RAINFOREST

Uganda is a beautiful country that was once called the 'Pearl of Africa'. The people are said to be some of the friendliest in Africa. The scenery varies from lush fertile lands near Lake Victoria, to dense tropical forests and mountain ranges bordering the Democratic Republic of Congo, to the semi-desert landscape of the north where it meets Sudan.

Our first port of call is on the shores of the mighty Lake Victoria, the source of the White Nile, where the Owen Falls Dam has been built. We then visit the capital, Kampala, which has all the contrasts you would expect of an old colonial city mixed with a modern African one. While here we tour a museum to learn about the area. Our next stop is in the Semliki Valley where we visit the Ntandi people who live in the valley's tropical forests. We end this part of our journey travelling by truck through the forest's dark damp undergrowth.

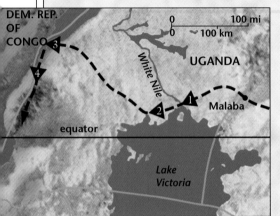

DEM. REP. OF CONGO

UGANDA

White Nile

Malaba

equator

Lake Victoria

0 — 100 mi
0 — 100 km

Owen Falls Dam

Just outside the town of Jinja is the Owen Falls Dam, a large hydroelectric station that uses the power of falling water to generate most of Uganda's electricity. It was finished in 1954 and now controls the flow of the White Nile as it leaves Lake Victoria. The original source of the White Nile, the Ripon Falls, was drowned when the dam was completed but you can still see the waters of the lake angrily tossing and turning where the falls lie hidden beneath the surface.

MUSEUM STOP

The Uganda Museum

Kampala, Uganda's capital, is a city returning to life after years of trouble and war. Today it is a city of wide avenues, green open spaces, bustling markets and trading streets. It continues to be rebuilt and will no doubt become a major African city. The Uganda museum has fascinating displays which tell us about local history and wildlife. The musical instruments section includes some that you can try. The instrument shown here is a type of xylophone. Our last stop in Kampala is at the Kasubi tombs, which house the bodies of the kabakas (kings) of the local Buganda people.

20

▼ The Ntandi of the Semliki Valley

In the forests of the Semliki Valley live groups of hunter-gatherers who are smaller than average human height. They are known as pygmies. Like their better-known relatives in the Congo or Amazon, they live off the plants and animals of the forests. Recently their population has declined due to human activities, particularly the cutting down of the forest. Unfortunately, tourists are a problem and their desire for souvenirs, such as locally made crafts, has helped destroy many groups' traditional way of life. The pygmies at Ntandi are used to tourists and we will briefly visit them rather than try and meet a relatively undisturbed group. It would not be respectful to force them to pose for photographs, so we leave all cameras and bags in the vehicle. The Ntandi men might show you the weapons they use for hunting, such as a bow and arrow or impressive spear.

INFORMATION PACK

Rainforests are the most diverse and complicated environments on earth, providing a home to more than half the world's plants and animals. An area of tropical forest the size of one football pitch often houses more insect species than you would find in the whole of the United Kingdom. Rainforests are made up of layers, with new seedlings at the bottom struggling to get enough light to start them on their upward journey. Above these are young trees pushing upward for their place in the canopy with the mature trees, some 35 metres above the ground. The biggest trees, called 'emergents', grow above the canopy, reaching heights of up to 90 metres.

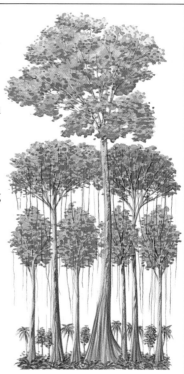

◀ Rainforest safari

To explore the rainforests we need a four-wheel-drive truck, powerful enough to drag its way through the muddy roads. Close to the equator it rains throughout the year, and in these forests new vegetation is always growing. You never know when you might have to stop to clear fallen trees or chop through overgrown lianas, hanging like ropes from the trees. The ground is uneven with the enormous roots of rainforest trees, holding them securely in the damp forest floor. Up in the canopy are plants called epiphytes, which cling to the branches. On the ground you may see beautiful plants and exotic flowers.

Next we set off on foot for the mountains.

THE MOON MOUNTAINS

We are now in the true adventure lands, on the edge of the great African rainforests. This area is of special importance for the unique plants and animals it protects and has long been an area of excitement to explorers and scientists. First we head into the Ruwenzori mountains. They are often called the Mountains of the Moon and were once thought to be the source of the river Nile.

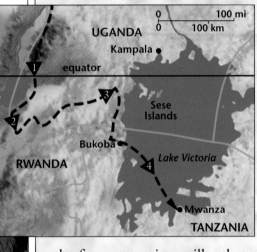

The Ruwenzori mountains offer some of the most spectacular trekking in Africa, with stunning views over the surrounding forests. Next we venture into the forests of Bwindi to visit some of the few mountain gorillas that are left in the world. Then we travel to Masaka where we see how people use the fish of Lake Victoria. Finally we continue our journey on board a ferry, hoping to catch sight of the impressive African fish eagle.

▼ The Ruwenzori mountains

Kasese is an old copper mining town (copper used to be one of Uganda's biggest exports) but the mines have long been closed and it is now a sleepy town of little interest to the traveller except that it is the starting point for treks into the Ruwenzori Mountains. These Mountains of the Moon, as they are often called, provide some excellent trekking, harder than anything else in the region.

The six-day trek takes us through tropical vegetation, across streams, past waterfalls, through bogs, over boulders and glaciers, and around lakes. A particularly memorable sight are the giant groundsel, heather, bamboo and lobelia plants that you come upon on the way. The mountain peaks that tower around you, some of them permanently snow-capped, are only for the most experienced climbers who carry necessary equipment to cope with the severe conditions.

◢ The gorillas of Bwindi

Bwindi National Park was formed less than ten years ago to protect one of the last remaining habitats of the mountain gorilla. There are thought to be less than 600 gorillas left in the world, and nearly half of them live in Bwindi and its neighbouring park, Mgahinga. Joining a small group, a guide takes us as close as possible to these magnificent creatures without disrupting their lives. It is a truly unique and memorable experience.

◢ Masaka

Masaka was badly damaged during the years of trouble in Uganda and although rebuilding has started several of the streets are still badly damaged. There is not much to do here, but it is a popular stop for travellers like us, making their way to Tanzania. It is also the nearest town to the beautiful Sese Islands in Lake Victoria. This group of 84 islands is totally unspoilt and offers a paradise for travellers to relax in.

As you pass through this area you will notice how much the local people rely on Lake Victoria for their living. Fish forms an important part of their diet so lots of fishing activities can be seen taking place. Of special interest is the way fish is smoked over a wood fire in order to preserve it. This is necessary because the fish would soon go off in the heat of the sun and there are very few household refrigerators to keep it fresh. You can sample some of the delicious smoked fish before you go.

◢ Lake Victoria and the fish eagle

The long bumpy road from Masaka brings us to the large town of Bukoba in Tanzania. It is a centre for the Tanzanian coffee industry, but more importantly it is Tanzania's second largest port, with ferry connections to other ports on Lake Victoria. We board the ferry to Mwanza on the southern shores of Lake Victoria and the journey gives us a chance to rest a little. It is important to keep one eye open as you might spot an African fish eagle soaring high above the lake. These magnificent birds, with their striking white heads, glide effortlessly in the air scanning the lake below in search of fish to eat. They often take fish left by other animals and have been known to chase other fish-eating birds, such as pelicans or cormorants, forcing them to drop their catch. But the fish eagle is most impressive when it decides to hunt for itself. Waiting until it spots a fish close to the surface, it swoops down at amazing speed and grabs the fish with its razor-sharp talons.

As the sun sets we approach the important port of Mwanza.

23

THE SERENGETI SAFARI

Mwanza is a busy port. Here people and goods from all over Tanzania travel to other ports on the shores of Lake Victoria. It is also the main settlement of the Wasukuma people – Tanzania's largest tribal group. For our first stop we will visit a museum that celebrates their culture.

Next we venture into the Serengeti National Park, one of the best game-viewing parks in the world. Then we head towards the Ngorongoro Crater, which was once a gigantic volcano. Today it is home to

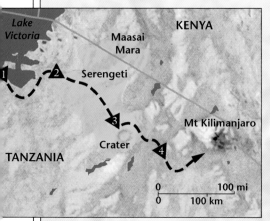

wildlife and to the Maasai herders, whose cattle share the rich grasses with the zebras and antelopes. We visit a village for our last stop and meet the Maasai people. They have been living in this

area since long before the first travellers arrived. Sadly their way of life and special culture are now threatened as Tanzania's population and wildlife conservation efforts take over their precious land.

MUSEUM STOP

Sukuma Museum

A short bus ride from Mwanza brings us to the Sukuma Museum where we learn how the local Wasukuma tribal group used to live. They are still the biggest of over 100 tribal groups in Tanzania today and are well known for their fine drums made of animal skins stretched over hollowed out timber. The different-sized drums produce different sounds. The museum also puts on a display of traditional music and dancing. It finishes with the Sukuma Snake Dance called the bugobogobo, which involves a live python!

2 Serengeti National Park

The famous Serengeti National Park is at the other end of the great wildebeest migration we saw in the Kenyan Maasai Mara. In fact the two parks join across the border to form one enormous wildlife sanctuary. Apart from the 1.4 million wildebeest, you will also see millions of other herbivores (plant eaters), such as zebras and giraffes.

lowly munching through the
savanna plains. If they all run at
once they may be trying to flee
from one of the carnivores (meat-
eaters), such as the lions, leopards,
and cheetahs, that prey on them.
It is quite unusual to see such a
chase as people have hunted the
big cats for many years and their
numbers have sadly dwindled.

◀ 3 Ngorongoro Crater

Ngorongoro was once a large
volcano, but the centre collapsed
inwards over two million years
ago to form a giant crater over
20 kilometres across. The
towering 600 metre walls of
the crater enclose over 30,000
animals, from dik-diks (tiny
deer) to the mighty elephant.
The bottom of the crater is
so big you could fit the city
of Paris into it!

Maasai village ▲ 4

The Maasai people have lived for hundreds
of years throughout the lands of Kenya and
Tanzania. They are herders and move their
cattle around the region in search of grass
and water. You may have seen a few of them
in the Ngorongoro Crater, as they are still
allowed to graze their animals there. In
many other places, however, modern life-
styles are forcing them to settle in villages
and abandon their traditional way of life.

Now we head east to Mt Kilimanjaro,
and then the Indian Ocean.

THE EAST COAST

The east coast of Africa is a mixture of fascinating history, breathtaking scenery, relaxing tropical beaches, and chaotic towns around important ports. We begin with a trek up Mt Kilimanjaro, which despite its permanent snow-cap is actually a dormant (resting) volcano which could erupt one day! The climb is worth the effort for the fantastic views it offers over the African plains – a memorable travel experience.

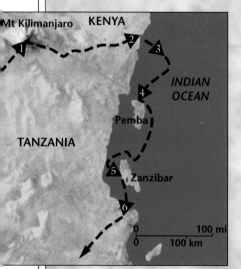

We cross back into Kenya to the port of Mombasa, where the first Europeans landed nearly 500 years ago. The city developed because of the Indian trade route and was once crowded with Arab trading boats called dhows. We take a dhow journey along the coast to the tiny island of Pemba, which although small is very important. The island of Zanzibar is our next stop. Here we explore the Arabic streets that were once the centre of the slave trade. Finally we travel to Dar es Salaam to learn about our ancient past.

▶ Mount Kilimanjaro

To climb Africa's greatest mountain we travel near the Kenyan border, and take a five-day trip on the Marangu trail. This takes us from the flat savanna to the snow-capped peaks, nearly 5,900 metres up. The highland forests on the mountain are home to many animals, including hundreds of black and white colobus monkeys. You might notice them sitting and watching you from the tree-tops.

▼ The Indian Ocean

We now take to the waters of the Indian Ocean and sail leisurely down the coast towards the spice island of Pemba. The palms that line the coast are loaded with big brown coconuts. Inside is a delicious coconut milk that is perfect to satisfy thirsty travellers. The dhow we travel in is a type of wooden boat that has been used for many centuries and was once the main form of transport for traders to the Middle East and India. Today there are fewer dhows and they are mainly used to take people between the mainland and the many small islands just off the coast.

▼ Mombasa

Mombasa is East Africa's most important port and links traders to the centre of Kenya, as well as Uganda, Rwanda, and Burundi. It was a trading post for Africans and Arabs for hundreds of years before the Portuguese arrived nearly 500 years ago and took over the town. The Portuguese built Fort Jesus as their central fortress but less than forty years later they were thrown out by the local people. Today Fort Jesus is filled with treasures from the many ships that visited over the years. Look through one of the cannon holes in the fortress walls and imagine what it was like defending the por

◀ Pemba

Most of the world's cloves are produced on this small island. Cloves are an important spice used in cooking and medicine. They are actually flower buds which are picked and laid out to dry in the sun on large mats made of coconut fibres. You will see cloves drying everywhere and notice the strong smell that drifts across the island.

◀ Zanzibar

Zanzibar, or Unguja as it is locally known, is another big producer of cloves but is better known for having been the centre of the East African slave trade and the Omani Muslims. Arab traders have used the island for hundreds of years and their influence can be seen in the type of buildings that are found on the island. Stone Town is the oldest part of Zanzibar and has hardly changed in the past 150 years. Walking through its narrow streets, with the people, children, and heavily laden donkeys, you get a feel for the way of life in Zanzibar. Many people still wear traditional Muslim clothing like the *kanzu* robes and embroidered caps worn by the men, and the black *bui-bui* gowns and concealing headscarfs of the women.

▥ MUSEUM STOP

▶ Dar es Salaam National Museum

In this museum you can learn about the early Arab settlers and the rise and fall of the Zanzibar slave trade. It also teaches us about the period when Germany, and later Britain, controlled what is today Tanzania. Among other fascinating relics are the two-million-year-old fossil remains of the Nutcracker Man. He was probably among the first human beings to have lived. The remains were found in the Olduvai gorge, near the Ngorongoro crater which we visited earlier on our journey (see page 25).

Now we board the TANZAM railway to the world's biggest game reserve.

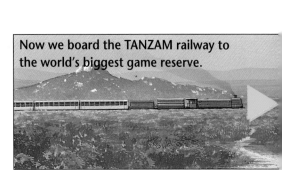

27

THE
LAKE OF STARS

The southern part of Tanzania that we have now reached is less developed than the northern and coastal areas. The people here are among the poorest in the world and live almost entirely on what they can farm from the land and trade with others. It is in this area that the enormous Selous Game Reserve, with its abundant wildlife and terrifying gorges, is found.

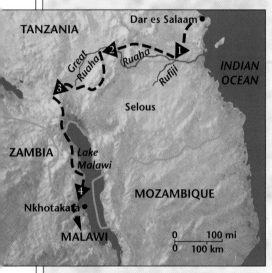

We cross one of these gorges as we pass through the reserve towards the Great Ruaha river for a close encounter with a crocodile. We then leave the wilderness and head for the market in the town of Mbeya on our way south to Malawi. On the shores of Lake Malawi we visit a fishing community. (Lake Malawi is so beautiful that the explorer Livingstone called it 'the lake of stars'.) Before moving on we discover more about the slave trade that used to take place here.

2 The Great Ruaha river

Ruaha National Park was formed in 1964. It is managed by Tanzania National Parks (TANAPA) who are protecting this large patch of wilderness. The Great Ruaha river is the centrepiece of the park and carves its way through the surrounding rocks carving out the deep gorges. It is a good place to see the crocodiles that lurk in the river waiting for their next meal to come along – make sure it is not you!

1 Stiegler's Gorge

The Selous Game Reserve is the biggest game reserve in the world. It is nearly three times the size of Wales! It is a wild place and has few visitors compared with other parks in the region. It is well known for its large elephant population of around 100,000, but perhaps more famous for Stiegler's Gorge, where the Ruaha and Rufiji rivers meet. There is a frightening cable car ride over the 100-metre-wide gorge for the brave traveller – but don't look down, it is 120 metres deep!

3 Mbeya

Once a supply town for the gold industry to the north, Mbeya is today an important transport centre for the railway between Tanzania and Zambia and the road network to Malawi. The region is very fertile and in the market you will see people selling apples, bananas, mangoes, and other fruits and vegetables grown in the area.

4 Lake Malawi

Throughout Africa many people fish in the lakes and rivers for extra food. The people around Lake Malawi have also taken to fishing to add fish to their diet. All along the busy lake shores you will see men mending their nets and putting fish into crates ready for cleaning and gutting. On the lake, boats prepare to cast their nets. Most of the fish is used for the families' own needs but some is transported to town markets to sell. There are over 200 species of fish in the lake and 9 out of 10 are only found in Lake Malawi. The cichlidae fish are the most common. They are called *chambo* and *utaka* by the local Nyanja people.

INFORMATION PACK

As we have already discovered during our trip to Zanzibar (see page 27), East Africa was the centre of a thriving slave trade in the eighteenth century. The slaves were taken from villages around Lake Malawi and the Mbeya region to the village of Nkhotakata on the shores of Lake Malawi. Nkhotakata became a major trading depot for the Arab slave traders. The slaves were then chained together and marched to Bagamoyo on the coast of Tanzania and across to Zanzibar. Up to 50,000 slaves a year were taken by the Arabs and traded in faraway countries, but thousands more died on the way.

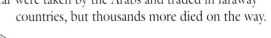

We continue along Lake Malawi's shores.

29

THE AFRICAN COPPERBELT

We paddle ourselves across the waters of Lake Malawi to Lizard Island for our first stop. Some travellers have found this a rather smelly island because it is littered with bird droppings. But the many birds and lizards that live there make it worth a visit. Just remember to hold your nose! We then leave Malawi and enter Zambia, a country rarely visited by tourists.

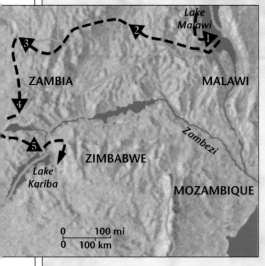

Our visit to Zambia begins with a trip to South Luangwa National Park. It has many of the animals that we have seen before but offers a rather special way of viewing them, as you will find out. Travelling north we visit one of the world's biggest mining centres, called the Great African Copperbelt. Next we arrive in Zambia's capital, Lusaka, and try some of the local food. We learn a little about Cecil Rhodes, who once controlled Zambia, before heading south towards Zimbabwe.

▼ Lizard Island

A short boat trip on Lake Malawi takes us to a small national park called Lizard Island. It is well known for its many lizards. One type of lizard to look for is the chameleon which changes colour when its moods alter. Experts can tell by its colour whether the lizard is angry or scared. The skin of some chameleons will also change to match the colours around them so they become camouflaged (hidden) from view.

▼ South Luangwa National Park

South Luangwa National Park appears to be like many of the parks we have visited, but here you can experience the African wildlife in different and exciting ways. The first walking safaris were tried here and they are still a thrilling experience. A walk alongside herds of zebras, antelopes, and elephants would make anyone's heart pound with excitement – or perhaps fear. But even more exciting are the moonlight safaris.

The bright spotlights of the safari jeep help to bring the night alive and give you a magical opportunity to see the nocturnal animals of Africa, like the bright-eyed bush baby, the quiet civet cat, and the large swooping owls. Night is also the best time to spot a leopard hiding in the moonlit grass as it waits to pounce on its unsuspecting prey. But at night the most noticeable thing is not the animal life, but the loud night-time noises. The chorus of clicking insects, croaking frogs, and laughing hyenas gets louder and louder as the sun disappears below the horizon.

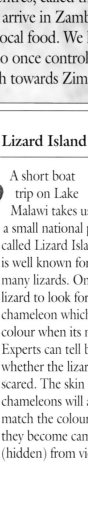

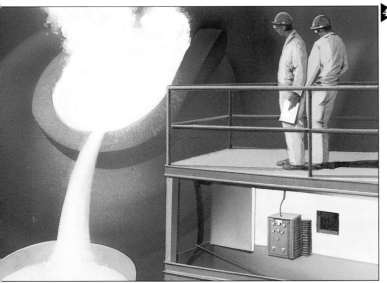

4 Lusaka

Lusaka is the capital of Zambia. Like many African capitals it developed because of the railway and the mining industries. Today it is the home of Zambia's president and government. The city-centre has flowering tree-lined streets. As with other big cities it is a wonderful place to try new food. A speciality in this area is crocodile tail, or perhaps you would rather try one of the many fresh fruits or vegetables grown in the surrounding fertile farmland.

▲3 The Great Copperbelt

Zambia has a band of underground rock across the middle of the country called 'the great copperbelt'. In this region hundreds of thousands of tonnes of copper ore (mineral rock) are mined every year. Zambia is the world's fifth biggest copper producer and many of its people rely on the copper industry for their living. We visit a smelting works in Ndola and watch ore being melted to get pure copper. The molten copper will be used to make pipes and electrical cables.

▽5 The upside-down tree

Now we have reached the Lake Kariba region where Zambia joins Zimbabwe. In this area you will notice giant trees called baobabs that are almost as wide as they are tall. Some people call them 'upside-down' trees because the branches look more like roots. They produce giant cream-coloured flowers, as big as dinner plates!

INFORMATION PACK

Cecil Rhodes (1853–1902) is an important figure in the history of southern Africa. Rhodes set off from the United Kingdom to go to Africa in 1870. Running a diamond mine in the South African town of Kimberley he soon became very rich. Rhodes later became a politician and spent the rest of his life trying to gain as much of Africa as possible for the British colonies. The colonies were lands controlled by British powers even though they were thousands of miles away. Rhodes did much of his work in Zambia and Zimbabwe. These countries were once called Northern and Southern Rhodesia in his honour.

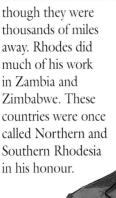

By crossing the top of the Kariba Dam we enter Zimbabwe.

GREAT ZIMBABWE

Zimbabwe is a country that has seen decades of conflict and turmoil. Trouble began in the colonial days of Cecil Rhodes and continued until Zimbabwe's independence in 1980. Today it is a country that is both safe and easy to visit, offering everything you could ask for, including spectacular scenery, lively cities, fascinating wildlife, ancient history, exciting adventure sports, and fantastic art and music.

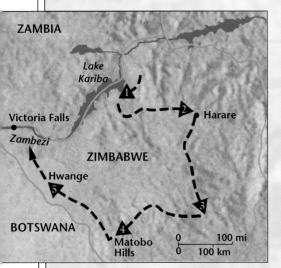

We begin our visit at the flooded forest of Lake Kariba, behind the Kariba Dam. We then head towards the capital city, Harare, calling in at a world famous sculpture park on the way. Next we go back in time as we view the ruins of Great Zimbabwe – once southern Africa's greatest city. The rock formations of Matobo National Park are our next stop before we climb the trees of Hwange for some of the best wildlife viewing in Africa.

▶ 1 Lake Kariba

Lake Kariba is an artificial lake formed in 1959 when the giant Kariba Dam was completed across the Zambezi gorge. The waters of the lake forced 50,000 Batonka people to leave their homes. Thousands of animals were moved in a famous rescue called Operation Noah. One of the most dramatic effects of the lake can be seen in the Matusadona National Park where hundreds of half drowned teak trees remind us of the forests that were once there.

INFORMATION PACK

The people of Great Zimbabwe lived throughout the surrounding area. Only the king, his family, and important tradesmen had houses in this great stone enclosure. Most of the community herded the king's cattle in far off pastures, following the rains in search of fresh grass. Near the great enclosure people worked with copper, iron, and gold to make tools and jewellery.

▶ 2 The Tengenenge sculptors

The Shona people of Zimbabwe are internationally known for their sculptures and nowhere is it better to see their skill than at Tengenenge. Here they have been joined by sculptors from Malawi, Zambia, and elsewhere to create one of the largest gatherings of African artists in the world. You can watch them skilfully carving the serpentine stone into traditional gods and spirits, or modern society scenes.

▶ 3 Great Zimbabwe

Great Zimbabwe was the most important stone settlement south of the Sahara desert. Built about 900 years ago by a powerful Shona kingdom it once had a population of 10,000. Eventually the kingdom lost its power. Historians are not sure why Great Zimbabwe became so powerful. Some think that it was the centre of an African gold trade. Others suggest it was the centre of a large cattle-herding civilization. The importance of the settlement is seen in the fact that its name, Zimbabwe (meaning 'stone house'), has become the name of the country.

4 The Matobo Hills

Matobo Hills National Park is famous for its spectacular granite rock formations. They were created millions of years ago as intense heat and pressure deep inside the earth forced molten lava to the surface where it cooled into hard rock called granite. Gradually the surrounding softer rocks and soils were eroded away, leaving the strange granite shapes we see today. Some of the smooth hills look like giant bald heads. (The name Matobo comes from the Ndebele word *amotobo* which means 'bald heads'.) There are thousands of smaller boulders scattered across the landscape like giant marbles. Most impressive of all are the balancing rocks – stacked on top of each other like acrobats in a circus.

The amazing beauty of this landscape has made it a spiritual centre for thousands of years. Even the colonial settlers were overwhelmed by it and Rhodes himself (see page 31) is buried here. Amongst the rocks there are caves to be discovered. They contain ancient rock paintings by people who once lived in the region.

5 Hwange National Park

Hwange National Park is the best park in Zimbabwe for seeing a wide variety of animals. It has a population of over 40,000 elephants, but if you are patient you will also see most of the other classic safari animals too. The best viewing opportunities are from the unusual tree houses, perched high in the branches overlooking the major water-holes.

The famous Rhodes train takes us north to Victoria Falls.

33

THE VICTORIA FALLS

When you step off the train at Victoria Falls station you know you have arrived somewhere special. Facing you is the grand Victoria Falls Hotel, built in 1914 for the wealthy colonial settlers. The small town of Victoria Falls has grown almost entirely because of tourism. The dramatic waterfalls and the exciting adventure sports attract tourists from all over the world. The money spent by the tourists provides an important income for local people.

Victoria Falls, one of the natural wonders of the world, is our first stop. After seeing the Zimbabwe side, you could cross the railway bridge to the Zambian side and see daring tourists doing bunjee-jumps 111 metres into the Zambezi Gorge below!

Back on firmer ground we visit the statue of the explorer David Livingstone, and learn how the falls were formed, before heading for adventure ourselves on the frothy white waters of the Zambezi.

ZAMBIA

ZIMBABWE

Zambezi

Falls

Livingstone

ZIMBABWE

BOTSWANA

ZAMBIA

0   100 mi
0   100 km

► ## The Victoria Falls

Approaching the Victoria Falls you hear the almighty rumble of cascading water and see plumes of spray dancing in the air, long before you arrive. It is easy to understand why the local people call the falls Mosi-oa-Tunya which means 'the smoke that thunders'. Livingstone gave them the name 'Victoria', after Queen Victoria. The falls stretch 1.7 kilometres across the Zambezi gorge and plunge 100 metres to the fierce waters below causing a permanent mist with beautiful rainbows. The mist has provided enough moisture for a small forest to grow nearby. This forest of

mahogany, ebony, and fig trees is home to monkeys and small buck. The forest and the falls are protected and lie within the boundaries of a national park. Tourists often spend several hours exploring the falls but they also get very wet from the spray! To stay dry you can always take a helicopter, aeroplane, or microlight flight over the falls.

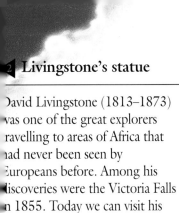

Livingstone's statue

David Livingstone (1813–1873) was one of the great explorers travelling to areas of Africa that had never been seen by Europeans before. Among his discoveries were the Victoria Falls in 1855. Today we can visit his statue which looks out over the falls, and across the border to Zambia. There lies Livingstone, a town named after him.

How were the Victoria Falls created? The heating and cooling of the earth's surface millions of years ago created areas of strong and weak rocks. As the Zambezi river flowed over these it found a crack in the weak rocks and began to wear them away. The pressure of the water rushing through a small crack over millions of years continued the erosion. Eventually the Victoria Falls and the gorge that we see today were formed. Today's falls are actually the eighth set – the first falls were once 8 km downstream.

The Zambezi river

The Zambezi river is 2,700 kilometres long and flows from northern Zambia through Namibia, Botswana, Zimbabwe, and Mozambique before entering the Indian Ocean. The river is normally wide and slow, but after tumbling over the Victoria Falls into the Zambezi gorge it becomes wild and frothy as it rushes over rocks and bounces off the edges of the gorge. These waters, known as rapids, are good for exciting outdoor sports like white-water rafting. Joining a group which has all the right equipment is the easiest and safest way to experience the rapids, which have been given such names as Big Eddy, Muncher, and Stairway to Heaven.

We travel on to one of the world's greatest wetlands.

THE OKAVANGO DELTA

We have now reached Botswana – a country split in two. The central and southern part is hot and dry with the Kalahari desert taking up most of the area. The north is more fertile, with large areas of savanna and the wetlands of the Okavango Delta. Botswana's population of 1.5 million is tiny compared with the 28 million in Kenya, a country of the same size. You are more likely to see animals than people in Botswana.

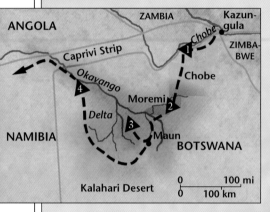

Crossing from Zimbabwe we follow the Chobe river. The huge herds of elephants here are a bit of a problem because they trample down and destroy the vegetation as they roam around. We continue into the Moremi region where the savanna bush gives way to the lush wetlands of the Okavango. Here we visit a termite colony before arriving in Maun and flying to a camp in the delta for a boat trip through a maze of papyrus channels. Finally we head north by river towards Namibia, looking at the colourful, shoreline bird-life on the way.

▶ 1 The Chobe river

The Chobe river drains the great wetlands that form the border between northern Botswana and a thin piece of land belonging to Namibia, called the Caprivi Strip. The Chobe joins the Zambezi river at Kazungula, and when you stand on the banks there you can see four countries at once: Botswana, Namibia, Zambia, and Zimbabwe. The Botswana side of the river is rich in wildlife, including enormous elephant populations. You may see herds of up to 500 with their young.

▶ 2 Moremi Wildlife Reserve

The area known as the Moremi Wildlife Reserve is rich in wildlife because it has both wetland and dry land environments. As you travel through the reserve looking for animals it is easy to forget the native insects, which can be just as interesting. For example, termites live throughout the dry lands of Africa in mounds that are up to 6 metres tall. These nests, called termitaries, are home to over a million termites. They are made of earth mixed with saliva (from the termites' mouths) which then bakes in the sun. Inside there are miles of tunnels leading to different parts of the nest. Most lead to the ruling queen termite, who is guarded by fierce soldier termites. She is the only termite that breeds, and produces up to 30,000 eggs a day. These are looked after by thousands of worker termites. The large number of eggs she carries means she is up to 20,000 times bigger than the other termites and weighs so much she cannot move!

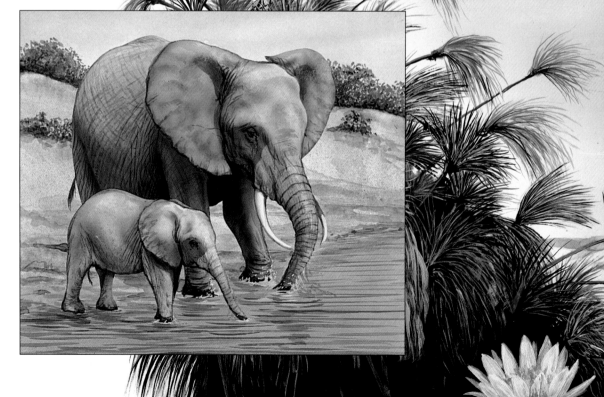

▼3 The Okavango Delta

Once a year rains fall in the highlands of Angola and rush down the 1,300 kilometres of the Okavango river towards Botswana. Unlike most rivers, however, the Okavango never reaches the sea. Instead it splits into a maze of thousands of channels which spill out towards the Kalahari desert before disappearing into the hot sands without a trace. The area in which it spreads is called a delta and the Okavango is the world's largest inland delta. Rich in plants and animals, and green as far as the eye can see, it is one of the most beautiful regions of Africa. To see this magnificent wilderness travellers take to the crystal clear waters in a wooden canoe called a *mokoro*. A guide pushes the canoe slowly along through the lily-covered water using a long pole. As you glide past the papyrus grass, ducks may fly off in alarm. But the braver wading birds, like the wattled crane, will probably ignore you and carry on feeding.

▼4 Birds of the Okavango

The Okavango river is a paradise for bird-watchers. By far the most beautiful species is the carmine bee-eater which lives in large groups on the riverbank, making its nest in the soft mud. It feeds on insects during flight and can spot a small fly from nearly 100 metres away.

INFORMATION PACK

The Okavango Delta is divided into two areas. The central area, close to the main river channels, is under water throughout the year and is known as perennial wetland. The outer areas, known as seasonal wetlands, are only flooded for certain times and in dry years they might not flood at all. The wildlife is concentrated in the perennial wetlands, but when the rains are good the seasonal wetlands spring into life with the arrival of fresh floodwaters. The wildlife of the delta could be threatened if neighbouring countries carry out plans to move water from the delta for human use.

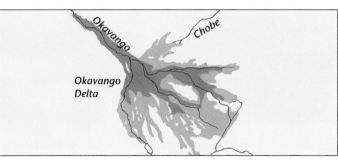

We take a jeep ride away from the wetlands and into Namibia.

THE SKELETON COAST

Namibia is generally a very dry country. The Namib desert, which we visit in the next stage of our journey, is one of the driest places in the world. We begin our visit to Namibia with a trip to the more fertile Etosha region in the north. Here you might see some of the thousands of animals that gather around the few patches of seasonal water that exist in Namibia.

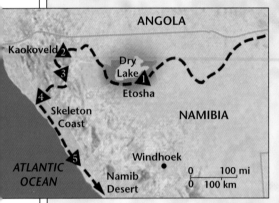

We then travel into Kaokoveld, a desert-scrub wilderness that is home to the striking Ovahimba people, who have hardly changed their way of life in 200 years. When you meet them you should respect their traditions and not take photographs as they find it rude and will expect you to pay them. The Skeleton Coast is our next stop. Here we take an exciting aeroplane safari for a bird's-eye view of the ghostly landscape. Finally we visit the Cape Cross Seal Colony to see thousands of Cape fur seals resting before their next fishing trip.

▶ Etosha National Park

Etosha means 'great white place of dry water' and refers to a large lake that dried up in the hot sun leaving white salty deposits. The famous Etosha wildlife lives not in this area but in the grasslands and woodlands around it. You might spot some of the rarer African animals such as the lynx cat, Damara dik dik (a type of deer), or black-maned lion. At seasonal waterholes you will certainly see more common species like the elegant gemsbok.

◀ Twyfelfontein

Twyfelfontein is known for its prehistoric engravings, which are at least 6,000 years old. The San people who once lived here made over 2,000 of these engravings by scratching the surface of the rocks. Most engravings are pictures of the animals that the San once hunted, such as giraffes. Many of these animals no longer live in the region.

▶ The Skeleton Coast

We take to the air now for a flight over the eerie Skeleton Coast. It was given this name because of the dangerous waters and thick fogs that confused sailors and often shipwrecked them onto the desert sands. Anyone washed ashore would not have survived long on the hot beaches or inland in the inhospitable Namib desert. Luckily there is little mist during our flight and far below you can see the wide beach with one of the many ships washed up on it. Despite the unfriendly environment there are some animals living in this region, including more than 350 savanna elephants that have adapted to the harsh conditions. Desert lions once lived here, feeding on washed-up whales and dolphins. But they are now extinct, the local people having killed them because they attacked their animals.

▶ Kaokoveld

This rugged place of desert mountains is often described as 'Africa's last great wilderness'. There are no roads and signposts, no towns, few people, and very little vegetation. It is the home of the nomadic Ovahimba people, who have remained isolated from modern life and continue to live and dress as they did 200 years ago. The women are particularly impressive. They wear goatskin skirts, and have their bodies and hair smeared with a mixture of butter, ash, and ochre (a paste made of clay and iron ore) to protect their skin from the burning sun. Most impressive of all is the jewellery they wear around their necks. It is made of iron, leather, and shells.

5 Cape Cross

Cape Cross has the biggest colony of Cape fur seals along the African coast numbering around 180,000. These seals are actually not seals at all, but relatives of the sea lion. The male adults weigh up to 230 kilograms and during the breeding season this weight nearly doubles. They feed in the Atlantic Ocean, eating over a million tonnes of fish, squid, and octopus every year – more than is caught by the Namibian fishing industry.

Next we head into the heart of the desert in a tough four-wheel-drive jeep.

THE NAMIBIAN DESERT

On this part of our journey we learn why the country is called Namibia (which means 'great arid desert'). The places we visit are some of the most remote and lifeless places on earth. Yet people and wildlife do live in them, as we discover. First, while driving through the moon-like landscape of the Namib-Naukluft Park, we look at the weird welwitschia plant. Next we head south into a great sea of sand and struggle to the top of an enormous sand dune.

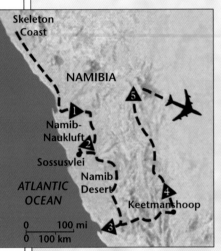

Despite the intense heat and lack of water and plants, some animals do survive here and we learn about them before moving on to the ghost town of Kolmanskop. Our next stop is the 'giants' playground', where we see strange rocks that were first formed millions of years ago and have continued to be eroded and shaped by the strong winds ever since. Finally we head to the centre and capital of the country, Windhoek.

The dunes might look lifeless but many unusual animals live there. The sidewinding adder (which moves sideways instead of forwards) has special eyes on top of its head to watch for prey when it lies buried in the cool sand. The toktokkie beetle collects precious moisture by pushing its bottom into the air to catch morning dew. The dew runs down its back into its mouth.

2 A sand dune sea

Sossusvlei is located in the middle of an enormous sand dune sea, which fills 32,000 square kilometres of western Namibia. Everywhere you look there are great rolling sand dunes like giant waves spreading out for around 100 kilometres in all directions. Around Sossusvlei the dunes are between 100 and 200 metres high and are a wonderful golden colour, but nearby some are even bigger and thought to be the largest in the world. Dunes like these are formed when sand, blown by the wind, gets caught behind a rock or plant. It then continues to build up to the mountains of sand we see today. The best way to see these dunes is to take a walk up one of them, but allow plenty of time and take lots of water because walking up steep sand is long and hard work.

1 Namib-Naukluft Park

Within the Namib-Naukluft Park you will discover a very strange plant called the welwitschia. This is specially adapted to the dry climate of the Namib region. The plant gathers water by catching the early morning mist on its leaves and channelling this moisture to the ground, near its roots. The welwitschia lives for a very long time, producing its first flowers when it has lived for 20 years. The biggest plants, measuring up to 1.5 metres tall and 2 metres across, are about 2,000 years old!

3 ▶ Kolmanskop

This town was built at the edge of the Namib desert and was the centre of Namibia's diamond industry until about 1920. The desert winds showered the town with sand until eventually, when the diamond industry declined, its people moved away. The desert has now taken over to create the sandy ghost town we see today.

4 ▶ Finger rock

Travelling north from Keetmanshoop we pass many strange rock formations. The area is called the 'giants' playground'. The shapes you see, like the finger rock shown here, were formed 170 million years ago when hot lava forced its way up through softer rocks which have since worn away.

5 ▶ Windhoek

Now we reach the capital of Namibia, which was founded in 1890 by the Germans who once ruled the country. They called it German South West Africa. The name Windhoek means 'windy corner' but you should be able to escape the desert winds in the wide green streets of the centre. Many of them are lined with German-style buildings and a large German Lutheran Church dominates the town centre. It is a good opportunity to pick up souvenirs from the Herero traders, who wear colourful traditional costume.

From Windhoek we board a plane and fly for 2 hours east to Johannesburg.

THE CITY OF GOLD

Now we arrive in South Africa, which is rapidly changing as it rebuilds itself following years of apartheid – the system where black South Africans were made to live, work, eat, wash, and even play separately from white South Africans.

From the airport we travel into Johannesburg, a city made rich from gold. The modern appearance of the city is very different to the township of Soweto, where we go next. Thousands of blacks were made to live in this area to provide a workforce for the rich white rulers. It is in Soweto that many of the violent struggles to end apartheid took place. Next we visit the lions in the famous Kruger National Park before heading south to a Zulu village, where we see traditionally made homes. South Africa's main mountain range is our last stop on the way to the East London Museum to see the oldest fish ever caught.

Kruger National Park

SWAZI-LAND

SOUTH AFRICA

Vaal

LESOTHO

Orange

Drakensberg

INDIAN OCEAN

0 100 mi
0 100 km

1 Johannesburg

Just over a hundred years ago a man called George Harrison was searching for his riches and stumbled across some strange looking rocks which he later discovered to be gold! This lucky find was reported to the government and soon afterwards thousands of people came to look for more. This started the biggest goldrush the world has known. The few tin shacks that sprouted up to house the first miners grew in number, soon creating the biggest mining and industrial centre in Africa: Johannesburg, 'the city of gold'. Today Johannesburg is a thriving modern city of tall office blocks, wide streets packed with cars, and about two million people rushing about their business. There are still gold mines on the edge of the city, but local industries also produce chemicals, metal products, textiles, and machinery. The city looks especially dramatic at night when the buildings light up like Christmas decorations.

2 Soweto

On the outskirts of the city of Johannesburg lies Soweto, which is short for South-West Township. It is made up of several towns that were set up by the white government to house the black Africans who worked for them. Today over a million people live in this maze of concrete bungalows and corrugated tin shacks. The conditions are often unhealthy and unsafe. It is hoped that in the 'new' South Africa life will improve, but as you pass through Soweto you see that life is still very hard for many people.

3 Kruger National Park

A visit to Kruger National Park, named after Paul Kruger, a former South African President, might not seem that interesting after all the parks we have visited, but it is a very special park because it was the first to be set up in Africa. Protected since 1898 it was an important example of how humans could look after Africa's treasured wildlife. It has much wildlife and is a good place to see lionesses looking after their cubs. You might choose to go on a wilderness trail – a three day walk, with a ranger as your guide.

◀ Kwazulu

The Kwazulu region to the south of Johannesburg is home to the great Zulu people. They were once Africa's most feared warriors and fought fierce battles with the British settlers. Today many Zulus live in the cities, but others graze livestock and grow crops in the area. Some still live in traditional Zulu homes made of wooden poles and mud. The poles are woven together, plastered with wet mud and left to bake solid in the sun. Finally, a thatched roof is added.

▲5 Drakensberg mountains

The Drakensberg range stretches 1,125 kilometres through eastern South Africa, and beyond. *Draken* is the Afrikaans word for 'dragon', and the mountains were given this name because according to African legend they are the home of dragons.

IIII MUSEUM STOP

6 East London

On the southeast coast we visit the museum in the town of East London. It has two rather unusual displays. The first is the only known dodo's egg in the world. The dodo was a large walking bird that became extinct (died out) 300 years ago. You will also see the first coelacanth ever caught alive. This primitive fish was thought to have disappeared 80 million years ago, judging by its fossilized remains.

We drive along the southern coast towards the Garden Route.

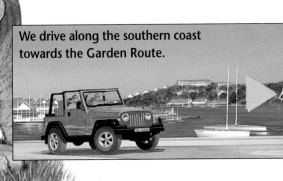

THE GARDEN ROUTE

The Cape Province is said to be the most beautiful part of Africa. The main city, Cape Town, is dominated by the spectacular Table Mountain which, with its flat top, really does look like a table. The mountain is a landmark for sailors, guiding them to Cape Town's safe harbour from up to 200 kilometres away. Cape Town is often called 'the tavern of the seas'.

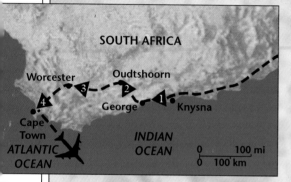

SOUTH AFRICA

Worcester Oudtshoorn
  3   2
         George   Knysna
  4
Cape
Town   INDIAN
ATLANTIC   OCEAN   0   100 mi
OCEAN   0   100 km

We approach Cape Town along the famous Garden Route and catch a train for one of the world's greatest railway journeys. We visit the home of over 90,000 ostriches before reaching the Karoo Botanical Gardens where we can relax and reflect on our journey. Our very last stop is in South Africa's oldest city, Cape Town (founded in 1652). From here we travel to the top of Table Mountain by cable car and look over the city below. Cape Town is the home of the South African parliament. We learn about Nelson Mandela's role in building a new South Africa before we head for home at the end of our exciting journey.

▼ 1 The Garden Route

As we near Cape Town we travel along the famous Garden Route, a narrow coastal strip that has lush green forests, grass-covered mountains, and millions of bright, scented flowers. Early visitors to the area, such as the French explorer Francois Le Vaillant, said that if nature lived anywhere it was here. The best way to view this enchanted garden is from the Outeniqua steam train which runs through the Outeniqua mountains. It is one of the world's greatest and most beautiful railway journeys – the steep zigzag tracks, dark tunnels, and impressive cuttings make it an unforgettable experience. Perhaps the most memorable sight is the railway bridge that spans the bay on the line between the towns of Knysna and George.

2 The Oudtshoorn ostriches

Near Oudtshoorn, special farms breed ostriches for their feathers, which are used in the fashion industry. These strange birds are the biggest on earth, growing up to 2.4 metres tall. They are flightless, but can run at 50 kilometres an hour if they need to escape. They also lay giant eggs, s big that one would be enough to make an omelette for 12 people!

3 ▶ Karoo Botanical Garden

Just outside the famous wine-producing area of Worcester is the Karoo Botanical Garden. Established in 1948 it contains many of the Karoo district's most beautiful plants. They include the deep pink Protea cynaroides, the queen of all flowers, which measures 30 centimetres across. It is South Africa's national flower.

INFORMATION PACK

In the 1950s and 1960s Nelson Mandela was an important leader in the African National Congress (ANC) which fought hard against white minority rule and the unfair apartheid system, which separated black and white people. The ANC was an illegal organization and in 1962 Mandela was sent to prison. There he became a symbol of the struggle to end apartheid. There was much rejoicing when he was eventually released in 1990, and in 1994 he was elected the country's first black president. He has become one of the world's most popular leaders.

4 ▼ Table Mountain

A cable car takes us to the top of Table Mountain in just six minutes, so make sure you are watching as the buildings disappear beneath you. The cable car service was opened in 1929 and today carries nearly 300,000 people every year. From the top of Table Mountain you have fantastic views over the city and port of Cape Town. You can also see Cape Point, where the Atlantic and Indian Oceans meet, and Robben Island, where Nelson Mandela was held in prison.

After our exhilarating journey we leave for home.

41

INDEX